I Keep Clean

Liz Lennon

W
FRANKLIN WATTS
LONDON•SYDNEY

Before eating ...

... and after going to the loo.

What do I need to do?

I need to wash
my hands.

So I keep clean!

I use warm water and lots of **soap.**

That keeps
germs away!

I've got a big sneeze coming.

I use a tissue.

Acchhoo!!

I wash my face. Because
I like to keep clean!

By the evening, I need another wash.

A bath makes my whole body clean.

How do I
look after my
nice smile?

I need to clean my teeth.

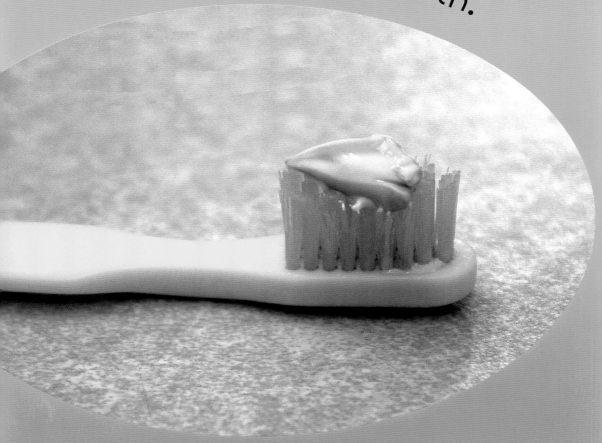

BRUSH! BRUSH!

I clean them
twice a day.

My hair needs washing too.

I wash it once or twice a week. Why?

Because it's healthy to be clean and it feels nice.

What do you use to keep clean?

Toothbrush

Soap

Nail brush

Tissues

Sponge

Nail clippers

Hairbrush

About this book

Keeping clean is an essential part of our daily lives. Looking at and talking about the pictures in this book is a good starting point to discussing hygiene. Do remember, however, that children shouldn't be afraid of getting dirty or muddy. Small children can inherit their parents' obsession with hand washing and an overuse of liquid soap/antibacterial gels is not good for young skin.

Washing hands It's easy for children to forget to wash their hands after going to the loo and before eating. Talk about germs, which are too tiny to see, but we know can make us ill. Washing our hands at these times helps to prevent germs making us ill. Discuss how we should use plenty of hot water and soap, and dry our hands thoroughly afterwards.

Using tissues Using a tissue when we need to blow our nose or sneeze helps to prevent germs spreading. If they can't get to tissues in time, sneeze into hands and wash them afterwards.

Washing our bodies Discuss why washing our whole body is important. What do they like about bath-time? Is it fun or a chore?

Cleaning teeth Children should use a pea-sized amount of toothpaste and be supervised to make sure they are cleaning all their teeth properly. Fruit juice and fizzy drinks can also cause enamel erosion.

Hair Some young children like having their hair washed and some hate it. Discuss what it feels like to have clean hair. What else do we do with our hair - e.g. brush/comb it, have it cut, wear hairclips or tie it back.

First published in 2011
by Franklin Watts

Copyright © Franklin Watts 2011

Franklin Watts
338 Euston Road
London NW1 3BH

Franklin Watts Australia
Level 17/207 Kent Street
Sydney, NSW 2000

All rights reserved.

Dewey number: 613.4
ISBN: 978 1 4451 0470 6

Printed in China

Series Editor: Sarah Peutrill
Art Director: Jonathan Hair
Series Designer: Paul Cherrill
Picture Researcher: Diana Morris
Consultants: Karina Philip
and Deborah Cox

Franklin Watts is a division of
Hachette Children's Books,
an Hachette UK company.

www.hachette.co.uk

Every attempt has been made to clear copyright. Should there be any inadvertent omission please apply to the publisher for rectification.

Picture credits:
Fotolia: Arvind Balaraman 18; Martin Green 10, 23cl; Olga Polyakova 19; Gelu Sorin Popescu 23br; robynmac 23tc; Alvin Teo 23cr; Alexey Ukhov 6; Serghei Velusceac 23tr; Joanna Zielinska 3. Istockphoto: Don Bayley 21; Chris Bernard front cover; Trent Chambers 8; Glenn Frank 20; Justin Horrocks 16; Kyu Oh 15; Juergen Sack 4. Shutterstock: Tim Arbaev 23bl; Chungking 22; Corepics 11; Dereje 12; Monkey Business Images 2, 14; Poulsons Photography 7; Raia 1, 13; Studio Online 5.